KAVANGO

With love to you,
Dick, this Christmas
of 1975, and with
best wishes for many
memorable nights
while reading this
book and recalling
our glorious S. W
Africa safari.

Mother

KAVANGO

ALICE MERTENS

PURNELL

CAPE TOWN · JOHANNESBURG
LONDON · NEW YORK

PUBLISHED BY PURNELL AND SONS (S.A.) (PTY) LTD
70 KEEROM STREET, CAPE TOWN

SBN 360 00233 1

LIBRARY OF CONGRESS CATALOG CARD No. 74-77973

REPRODUCTION BY HIRT & CARTER (PTY) LTD, CAPE TOWN
PRINTED IN SOUTH AFRICA BY ABC PRESS (PTY) LTD, CAPE TOWN
BOUND IN SOUTH AFRICA BY E. SEABROOK, CAPE TOWN

Acknowledgements

The Kavango territory is a remote area in South West Africa. There I met many kind people, people who have lived there for many years and from whose knowledge I profited. They helped me to make this publication possible.

I thank the government officials of South West Africa, especially Mr Marée, so many years commissioner for the Kavango territory.

I am very grateful to the late Dr Markus Zschokke, chief veterinary surgeon of this area, who introduced me to this untouched territory.

My thanks also go to Mr Fritz Wiers and his wife, whose kind hospitality I enjoyed; Mr Wiers showed me the whole of Kavango on his inspection tours.

I owe a debt of gratitude for the very great hospitality and help that I enjoyed at all the Missions, under Pater Fröhlich, Pater Baetzen, Pater von Roesmalen, Pater Förg, Pater von Lühlsdorf, Brother Uwis and Brother Laub, but I am specially thankful to the late Pater Noll and Pater Hartmann who have such a great knowledge of the country.

I gratefully recall the many nuns, who with their dedication have helped to develop and civilise the Kavango and whose achievements have gone unnoticed. They always welcomed me warmly in their midst, especially Sister Leopoldine with her good advice on many things (I retain memories of her beautiful Museum). Then there was 80 year old Sister Katharina, who has never returned home; she told me many things of the old times more than 50 years ago.

I remember with thanks Mr Potgieter of the road repair services, who was so helpful pulling vehicles out of the mud, and Lieutenant Steyn.

Also Pater Bonifaz, Chief Makushe and many other indigenous people, all eager to help.

I also thank Mrs Semmelink very much for the translation into German.

But most of all I am indebted to my friend Dr Maria Fisch, a doctor in this area for 16 years and therefore known to everybody. Without her tremendous encouragement, great knowledge and kind hospitality this book would not have been possible.

May it serve to show future generations, when most of these traditions have disappeared, what life was like in the Kavango territory.

Contents

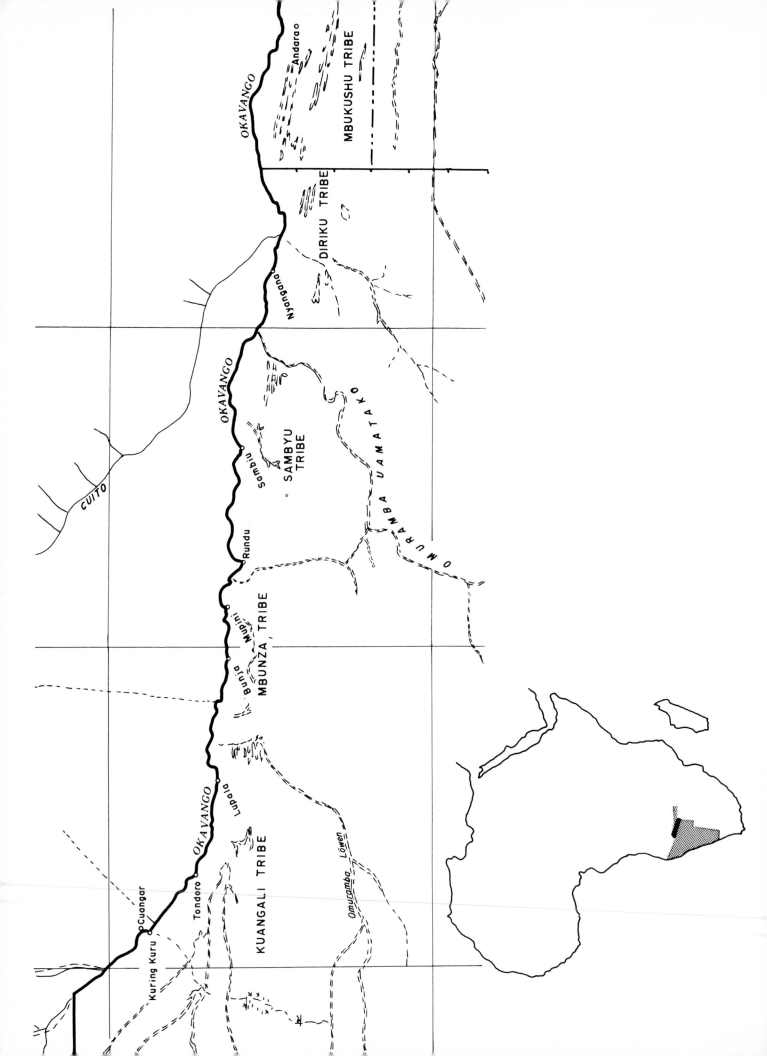

Introduction

'Tis better to be lowly born,
And range with humble livers in content,
Than to be perked up in glittering grief
And wear a golden sorrow.

Thus wrote Shakespeare in his chronicle of Henry VIII . . .
Which would beg the question: but where is such content? Where could such still be in this roaring age? In a world where, as Gerard Manley Hopkins once observed, 'all is seared with trade, bleared, smeared with toil, wearing man's smudge, and sharing man's smell? Where terror with its ten thousand faces has become endemic in ten thousand places' – all in the name of what was once so hopefully called: the pursuit of happiness?

Even when we have remarkably – how else could we survive? – adapted ourselves to such conditions, the thought would sometimes in moments of pause arise, whether in some far corner of the world there is no piece of earth which has escaped the sickness of the age. Some place where the soul-searing tensions of modern living, geared to both survival and progress, do not exist . . . Where men, still in reasonable numbers, live quietly, humorously, with sufficient food, shelter and opportunity for play . . . Beside a translucent, pollution-free river, ever flowing serenely . . . Where nature still obtains in pristine abundance, from the primitive denizens of the river, like crocodiles and hippopotami, to the sky-poised fish eagle sounding its haunting, lonely cry . . . Where a vast, game-rich hinterland still lies, for the use of stone-age people living with ancient earth intelligence off the roots and fruits and animals of the land . . . Where the sky in midwinter blue, tranquil as the river itself, arches infinitely overhead . . . Where in summer clouds gather like ancient men-of-war closing their ranks, to thunder majestically over a shimmering landscape . . . Where a cosmic hush then falls over the earth and the rain comes down like a heavenly curtain . . .

Is there yet such a land, where learning and the arts are still taken lightly, sufficient unto the day? Where ancient forms of tribal government have been gently synthesized with modern democracy, so that communities, on the whole, can live happy, ordered, well-provided-for lives?

This is neither fantasy; nor is it an exercise in the romantic. It is not Utopia. Such a corner of the world does indeed still exist. It is to be discovered where the Kavango River, descending from the central highlands of Angola, forms over a distance of more than 400 km the north-eastern border between that country and South West Africa. It is the land of the Kavango people.

Here is one of the most undisturbed, peaceful areas in the world. As a landscape it is also one of the most delectable: this broad, clear-running river, with its fertile flood plains, populated with trees of fine proportions, capable of excellent crops. In an area of more than 4 million hectares a variety of tribal and ethnic groups – less than 50 000 individuals – are contained. A *modus vivendi* has nevertheless evolved by which to each group is accorded what it reasonably needs and from each is expected what is reasonably due: all in the interests of good government.

Then this is Utopia . . .

Of course not; for Utopia lives only in the human mind. And besides, in this very mind the concept has become associated with gross national product and material advancement. In the cold perspectives of the prophets of growth, the Kavango would be regarded as a backward area. In the fiery perspectives of those who would first and last seek the political kingdom, it would be seen as vestigial colonialism. To those who now for more than two centuries have been rooted in this river land, it is *patria*, beautiful, bountiful and benign.

Finds of paleolithic and mesolithic stone implements and artifacts indicate that the Kavango was inhabited by humans some 80 000 years ago. The main body of the present five tribes, moving southward along the Kwando River – an arm of the Zambesi – reached the area c. 1750: a hunting expedition, according to legend, having discovered the Kavango itself. But it was the Herero people, also migrating southward from their former central, southern African lands, who gave the name. A large river on the right, they called Okunene: the big arm. A similar river on the left they called Okavango: the left, or little hip.

But for the world at large the river was only discovered in 1860 by the Anglo-Swedish pioneer and explorer – the most widely travelled and articulate in the fascinating story of South West Africa in early times – Charles John Andersson.* He had undertaken a hazardous journey from Walvis (Walwich) Bay, attempting to reach the Kunene via the wild and almost unknown Kaokoveld. A series of accidents and hardships caused him to abandon his direct route northward and turn inland. Eventually reaching the Omuramba wa Matako, intending to outflank a hostile Ovamboland, travelling hopefully, if arduously, he one morning perceived on the far distant horizon a distinct dark blue line.

'"Ah ha!"' he later recorded in his chronicle of the journey, 'I

---

*There is some evidence that a Portuguese trader, B. F. Brochado, visited the Kavango in 1851. In 1856 the hunter/explorer Frederick Green was at Andara (Libebe) with Professor Wahlberg, who was later killed by an elephant near Lake Ngami. Andersson, however, was the only one to record his journey and was therefore the effective discoverer.

exclaimed to myself, "in the valley of which that line evidently forms the border, there is surely something more than a periodical watercourse." A few minutes afterwards, catching a glimpse of an immense sheet of water in the distance, my anticipation was realized to its utmost. A cry of joy and satisfaction escaped me at this glorious sight. Twenty minutes more brought us to the banks of a truly noble river, at this point at least 200 yards wide. This was then in all probability the Mukuru Mukovanja of the Ovambo (*the Kunene*), which these people had given us to understand flowed westward. Taking it for granted that their statement was in this respect correct, I had stood some time by the water before I became aware of my mistake. "By heavens!" I suddenly exclaimed, "the water flows toward the heart of the continent, instead of emptying itself into the Atlantic!"'

Andersson, for many weary months, had been searching for the Kunene, and now he had discovered the Kavango.

It remains one of the strangest, most intriguing rivers in the world.

It gathers its clear silt-free waters in central Angola. Strengthened by the equally limpid stream of its main tributary, the Kuito, it forms for almost half its length the north-eastern border of South West Africa. Near Andara it then cuts through that most unusual tongue of land reaching towards the Zambesi, the Caprivi. It finally spills into the vast marshes of the Kavango in north-western Botswana, there to gradually lose its life in the Kalahari sands. In literature it has been seen as a symbol of human life being slowly dissipated and shallowed in the pursuit of an impossible ideal. Most remarkably, and with what one might call sweet irony, this very death of a great river might still serve to redeem one of the richest and last remaining wild life areas in all Africa; these very marshlands which in history had always been regarded as useless: in fact as a source of malarial infestation. The marshes of the Kavango may yet become one of the great bird sanctuaries of the world, and an earner of much needed foreign exchange for Botswana.

The middle reaches of the river, forming the South West African/ Angolan border, have always been a haven – in the human sense. Here, as indicated, the immigrants from central southern Africa came to rest in the mid-18th century. Here, too, that most singular odyssey in the history of western man, the Thirstland Trek, came temporarily to rest during the late seventies of the previous century. This group of well-established farmers from the western Transvaal had set out from the Crocodile River in various groups during the mid-seventies: following the sun, in search of what they believed would be their ultimate Calvinist 'Land of Rest' – Beulah. The journey lasted some seven years and the way – across the Kalahari Thirstland; past the fever marshes of the Kavango; through the bush country of northern South West Africa; through the Kaokoveld; to where they eventually settled on the highlands of the Sera da Chela in southern Angola – was marked by the graves of their loved ones.

In 1878, after suffering terribly in the so-called Tebraveld west of the Kavango marshes, they eventually reassembled near Andara: at Leeu Pan and Olifants Pan, south of the river. At the latter place hunters in the employ of Hendrik van Zyl, king of the great elephant hunters of the 19th century, had the previous year, on a Sunday afternoon, shot 103 elephants. For many months afterwards the river people had feasted off their dried flesh. A tree on the Pan for many years bore the record of this slaughter and what came to be known as the Van Zyl battle.

It was here at the Kavango that the Thirstlanders met Will Worthington Jordan, who had been at the river on a hunting trip. He not only attended the ill – he was widely known for his medical knowledge – but offered to take the Trekkers into war-torn Damaraland, so that they could establish the nucleus of a civilized state there. War finally disrupted his plans, and he had to lead them to Angola instead. As a Cape Coloured man, serving the most fundamentalist of the Boers as guide, counsellor, and friend, he finds a unique place in history. Who knows, perhaps it was the benign atmosphere of the Kavango itself which had made this strange friendship possible. Jordan died some six years later as a martyr to the Boer cause, after having brought them back from Angola to settle in the embryonic republic of Upingtonia, around Grootfontein: Otjovande Tjongue as it was then called.

But the perennial haven which the Kavango afforded was for those who had settled there two centuries earlier, or more. Five different tribes – the VaKwangari, the VaMbunza, the VaSambyu, the VaDciriku, the HaMbukushu – gradually settled on both sides of the river. Among these five Kavango tribes there are also later immigrants from Angola valled VaNyemba. Not only the various original tribes, but also the newer immigrants live in separate settlements.

In the interior of the Kavango territory, !Khû and Khoé (Mbarakwengo) Bushmen still lead their ancient stone age life: living in the age old ways off the bush and tree covered land, with only a few permanent settlements.

The Kavango people, in their separate tribal areas along the river, subsist by virtue of both horticulture and animal husbandry. The women, using the hoe, till the fields. They also gather the crops. The men tend the animals. In the forests bordering the river there is a great variety of fruit-bearing trees. In the veld there are flying ants, luscious caterpillars, locusts, all containing a rich assortment of fats, proteins and carbohydrates. Collecting this bounty, as well as hunting and fishing, provides the Kavango people with the kind of diet modern industrial societies would package expensively and sell as health foods.

This African Eden . . .

So one might well conclude. But the history of South West Africa during the 19th century, as Heinrich Vedder has recorded in a monumental piece of historical writing,* is one of internecine warfare, mainly between the northern Hereros and the southern Namas. By the end of the seventies a stage of mutual destruction was almost reached.

The Ovambos in the far north had also been constantly engaged in bloody conflict. Only the people of the Kavango, knowing, at times, nothing more than minor violence, seemed to prosper steadily. The organized raids, the systematic warfare which characterized so much of South West African history, was almost completely absent here. In the distant east, during the second quarter of the 19th century, more than a million people had died on the South African highveld with the expansions of the Zulu Kingdom. Only along the shining, far, inland river, the Kavango coursing towards its vast, marshy delta in the northern Kalahari, was there nothing even remotely similar.

For this there may well genetically be reasons. But environmentally too, tranquility was favoured. This is a blessed land . . .

But the old order changeth . . . It changes even here in the Kavango. Ancient tribal customs, such as that of clan membership, determined by matrilineal relationship and the rule by chiefs within the same genetic system, have been subtly allied to representative rule by a council of ministers. The subsistence economy of the past is no longer wholly acceptable to the young men of the tribes. They prefer, like the rest of black Southern Africa, to go off and earn money in the industrially developed areas.

The Christian mission, too, established itself, after initial difficulties: the Catholic Congregation of the Oblates of the Virgin Mary in 1909; and the Finnish Protestant Mission in 1926. The fundamental Kavango belief in Karunga (or Nyambo, among the Mbukushu) as a transcendent god, opened the way for the Christian message. The river too – the Kavango – has produced a humble, deeply religious people.

Education, like development in many other fields, sponsored by the mandatory power which is South Africa, has gone strongly ahead. There are now nearly 100 schools in the territory, including a modern secondary and technical school at Rundu, and a new secondary school at Katere. Roads, medical services, agricultural aid have been improved everywhere. The far distant world of the 20th century is now much, much nearer than it was even a decade ago.

It is the human story everywhere. The process of acculturation proceeds relentlessly everywhere. The most we can hope for is to humanize it in every possible way, retaining enough of the old in the acceptance of the new: conserving what time itself has proved to be of lasting value. In that far distant, shining land of the Kavango it is to the credit of all – mission people, medicos, government officials, social scientists, anthropologists, historians that they have recognized this: that, with great integrity and dedication, they are assisting a people to advance materially, governmentally, and yet save their souls.

*South West Africa in Early Times (London, 1938)

This, too, is the meaning of this photographic record by a true artist of the camera. Alice Mertens' photo essay on the Kavango is more than just a record. It is also a tribute and an interpretation. In its finest moments it is, like all art, a revelation.

W. A. de Klerk

1. A peaceful, slow flowing river, the Kavango is untouched by exploitation as it flows south-eastward, and disappears into the swamps in Botswana.

2. Chipped teeth add to the beauty of a Kavango woman. The military buttons worn on the temple were once the badge of royalty. Now they are a sign of wealth.

3. A Mbukushu woman's hair is lengthened with string or sisal and rolled with fat into long tresses. The front of her hair is plastered with mud and fat. A root is bound on top with sisal and everything decorated with beads and cowrie shells. A fat ox is paid for the latter.

5. A typical Kavango family scene. Children gather round the three-legged pot while their mother stirs the stew with a stick.

4. A young Kavango boy of the Mbukushu tribe. His father is a minister in the present Kavango parliament.

6. Fishing is popular and the catch provides part of the Kavango diet. Small fish are dried, ground, and added to the Mahango pap — a porridge the Kavangos eat.

7. Often it is the children who fish — both boys and girls.

8–9. Here some village boys enjoy a race across the river.

10. Kavango children help with the daily chores. These two small girls fish for the evening meal.

11. The fishing basket called 'Shikuku' is constructed with flattened reeds fastened with sisal, the thin branch of a tree forming the rim.

12–13. A Kavango woman's wealth is reflected by the number of beads and cowrie shells incorporated in her hair-do.

13

14. Mothers often start lengthening the hair of their little girls at an early age.

15. A pretty Kavango mother comforts her crying child.

14

16. The Kavango river near Andara Mission.

17. Sunset on the Kavango.

18. Mahango is a drought resistant millet, similar to kaffir corn, growing on a cob. Here a Kavango woman picks the millet from the stalk.

19. Women take their homemade baskets filled with Mahango to a central collecting point.

20–21. As the heap grows, the men arrive with sledges, drawn by oxen, to collect the Mahango cobs.

18

22. The cobs are poured into the container made from reed mats. The bottom of the sledge is made from the fork in a tree trunk.

23. The boy who will lead the oxen home, squats on the ground as he waits.

24. Beautiful young girl carries a basket of palm leaves filled with Mahango cobs.

25a. A woman fishing in the still clear waters of the river.

25b. Women and children return home from a fishing expedition.

25a

25b

26a. A young boy leads the oxen, pulling the heavily laden sledge to the kraal.

26b. The young oxen are used for joy rides.

27. At the kraal the sledges are unloaded.

29. ▲ The sledge is tipped over, and the cobs are unloaded.

28. ◀ African still life. The fork, baskets and mat are made by hand.

30. Women club the Mahango off the cobs with wooden pestles.

31. Young girls stamp the Mahango millet into fine flour, using wooden pestles and mortars.

32a. The threshed Mahango is taken to a hut to be stored.

32b. Melons are stored near the family hut.

33a. Once a fortnight a doctor visits the settlements in the Omuramba Wamatako district.

33b. A herd boy tends the cattle grazing on the lush green grass.

33c. Windmills and concrete watering troughs are new in the Omuramba district.

33d. New fields are being opened up in the Omuramba.

32a

32b

33b

33a

33c

33d

34. An old woman can still be useful for cracking open Manketti nuts.

35. The late afternoon sun lights up a typical village scene — women squatting around a small fire with their children, while a dog sniffs the sand.

36. A young Kavango girl, her hair lengthened with sisal, takes her turn at the cooking pot.

37. Big sisters look after little ones, which they do with loving kindness and without grudge.

38. Each year a 'Corpus Christi' Procession is held. For this a statue of the Madonna is borrowed in Angola and for its return two days later the boat is beautifully decorated.

39. The Procession, with the small madonna in the boat and the late Pater Fröhlich accompanying it, is floating down the river. A magnificent sight which all the natives along the river enjoy.

40. The Popa Falls, glistening in the sunlight.

41. The colourful River Procession.

42. The small Madonna, carved in wood, was made in Italy.

43. A choir boy, proud of his position, is one of the paddlers in the procession.

44. The Nyangana Mission Church on a Sunday.

45. Nyangana, the oldest mission on the Kavango, founded in 1908, seen across the tranquil river, is famous for its large school and hospital.

46. Andara Mission is named after the chief who gave his permission for its establishment in 1909.

47. The large basilica at Tondoro Mission on Sunday. For 14 years Pater Noll had bricks and the tiles for the roof made in spare time. When they had ½ million bricks, the church was built after his design, copying a church in Münster-Schwarzach in Germany.

48a. School is out!

48b. Sunday service in Sambyu church near Rundu.

49. Tondoro Mission Church on Sunday.

48a

48b

50. The 'Shanjime' rock near Andara Mission. In the old days adultresses, bound hand and foot, were thrown to the crocodiles from the rock on which the boy is standing.

51. Near Andara the Kavango river has to squeeze its way through rocky outcrops. Its flow here becomes faster and more turbulent.

52. Chiefs' Island, near Andara Mission, where all the chiefs of the Mbukushu tribe lie buried. Only the six men who take a chief's body across the river to bury it, are allowed to set foot on the island.

53. On this rocky island is a large cave in which the chiefs of the Mbukushu tribe hid their wives and children during times of war. The boy is standing next to the entrance.

54. Makushe wa Kangwa, chief of the Mbukushu tribe.

55. Shashipapo, chief of the Dciriku tribe, near Nyangana, is a minister in the Kavango government.

56a. Kavango woman with an elaborate hair-do.

56b. Kavango woman with bead necklace.

56c. Nyemba woman with scarification and chipped teeth.

56d. Young Nyemba girl with tightly plaited hair.

57a. Skirt made from an animal skin, with cowrie shells and beads.

57b. Skirt with two wide bands and numerous single strands of beads.

57c. Large beads were used to make this attractive skirt.

57a

58. Old man from the Sambyu tribe.

59. A headman from the Dciriku tribe. He is one of the most respected members of the tribe.

60. Sambyu Mission has the most beautiful vegetable and flower gardens along the Kavango river. While making these gardens many stone implements and artefacts such as hand-axes were found. Pater Hartmann collected quite a few, half of which are in the museum in Windhoek and the other half in the museum of his old cloister in Weingarten, Germany.

61. Sambyu is the only mission along the Kavango river that can boast a fine museum. These beautiful exhibits were collected by Sister Leopoldine.

62. Kavangos are an artistic people. Here a young boy models an ox out of clay gathered from the river bank.

63. These Kavango boys admire their handiwork: oxen, dogs, giraffe, a tortoise and a farmer.

64a. This wooden chain was carved, all in one piece, out of the trunk of a tree.

64b, c, d. Three wooden stools carved out of tree trunks. The mask-like faces are typical of African carvings.

65a. This young boy makes a clay ox to show his classmates.

65b. Oblivious of the camera, a young girl fashions a clay pot.

65c. Carrying tinned fish to your father is fun if you can make a bracelet out of grass on the way.

64b

64a

64c

64d

66. Girls concentrate on making pots and stamping blocks out of clay.

67. The sensitive fingers of this small girl model a stamping block.

66

68. A fairly good living can be made from selling carvings to curio shops in South Africa and abroad. The Bantu Investment Corporation buys the carvings from the Chokwe and Nyemba tribes and distributes them to the curio shops.

69. Beautiful chairs and tables are carved by hand.

70. This craftsman displays his wares along the road in the hopes of catching the attention of a passing tourist.

71. Summer rains can be torrential in the Kavango. The Kavangos keep their carvings under canvas.

72a. An old man sharpens his knife on a stone.

72b. A Nyemba tribesman puts the finishing touches to a chair.

72c. He displays his wares outside his hut, which is made with wooden poles and mud.

73a. This Nyemba tribesman begins carving what will eventually be a stool.

73b. Carving a mask.

73c. Putting the finishing touches to a stool.

73d. Three wooden buck on display.

72a

72b

72c

73a

73b

73c

73d

74a. Drum carved out of a tree trunk, has an animal skin stretched tightly over the top.

74b. A dugout canoe being paddled down river by slave raiders. In the canoe are the slaves.

74a

74b

75a

75a. A handmade basket, of palm leaves, for collecting mealies.

75b. An almost flat basket, for winnowing the grain.

75c. This long basket is used only by the Sambyu tribe, to sift flour.

75b   75c

76. An old smithy shapes some tools.

77. The iron is softened on glowing hot coals. They are heated by using bellows, the way it has been done for hundreds of years.

78. ▲ Sadly, the art of pottery is dying out today. Here an old potter skilfully fashions a huge beer pot.

79. ▶ Reed mats feature prominently in the daily life of the Kavangos. They sleep on reed mats and use them as containers on their sledges. Reeds growing along the river are cut, split open, flattened and left to dry. They are then woven into mats.

80a. Baskets are used daily as well as being sold to tourists.

80b. Banana fronds form the background to this picture of concentration and skill.

81a. Nimble fingers are an essential in basket making.

81b. A large, nearly completed basket made of palm leaves.

81c. If you haven't a pair of scissors, then teeth are the next best thing to end off a section.

80a

80b

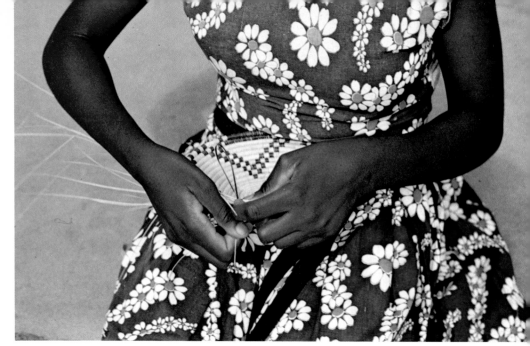

81a

81c

82. ▲ Young girls on a mission station learn the old art of basket making in addition to their schooling. A pail of water is handy for keeping the sisal pliable.

83. ▶ Making their own clothes on sewing machines is one of the skills the Sisters teach the Kavango girls.

84—85. The bush is dense, almost jungle-like in places, on the way to the Kavango Swamps.

86. ◀ Bushman women look for nuts in the Manketti forests.

87. ▼ A small Bushman girl squats on her haunches.

88a. A Bushman woman returns home after collecting roots and bulbs, her baby secure in an animal skin pouch.

88b. Bushman women in the Kavango also often lengthen their hair.

89a. A Bushman woman in her hut of reed mats.

89b. A young Bushman washes himself in the clear, still waters of the Kavango river.

89c. A Bushman child washes his face in the plentiful water.

87

88a

88b

89a

89b

89c

91. ▲ This fat little Bushman baby is already lovingly decorated with beads.

90. ◀ Wrinkled old Bushman woman is richly decorated with beads.

92. ▲ The Bushman hunter takes careful aim with his bow and arrow, which he made himself.

93. ▶ The full grown Bushman hunter is small compared to the two teenage boys. The average Bushman height is 150 centimetres.

95. ▲ The cemetry of Andara Mission. Under the Baobab tree are the crosses of the first two missionaries to reach the Kavango, in 1907. They trekked for many weeks under tremendous hardships to die soon after their arrival from blackwater fever.

94. ◀ Elegant Makalani palms thrive on the open plains near Tondoro Mission.

96a. Dark rain clouds gather over a village.

96b. Roads are soaked in water.

96c. Many roads are impassable and vehicles become stuck in the mud.

96d. Dugout canoes are the safest form of transport in the rainy season.

97. Rundu is the capital of the Kavango.

96a

96b

96c

96d

97

99. ▲ Chief Makushe who shot the hippo, takes off the tail of the hippo. This is cooked and eaten by his favourite wife.

98. ◀ This hippo has been shot by a chief. It's the sole right of the chiefs of the Kavango to shoot one hippo a year.

100. ▲ The eldest councillor then starts carving up the hippo.

101. ▶ The men and children watch intently. There will be lots of good food once the carving is over.

102–103. The Kavango river near Andara. This is close to the place where the hippo feast was held.

104. ▲ A drummer beats out a message that there will be a big feast that night.

105. ▶ Dugout canoes begin arriving from near and far. Some have to brave the rapids to partake in the feast.

106. Beer is prepared and carried to the chief's kraal in these calabashes. Leaves stop up the opening, so that the precious liquid will not spill.

107. The beer is poured out into large cast iron pots. Everyone can fill their mugs from these.

108. The men gather round as the hippo is carved up.

109a. The eldest advisor makes the first cut.

109b. Younger men take over the hefty task of cutting up the massive animal.

109c. In the evening the women of the tribe clap their hands and sing.

109d. A little boy eats his first hippo meat.

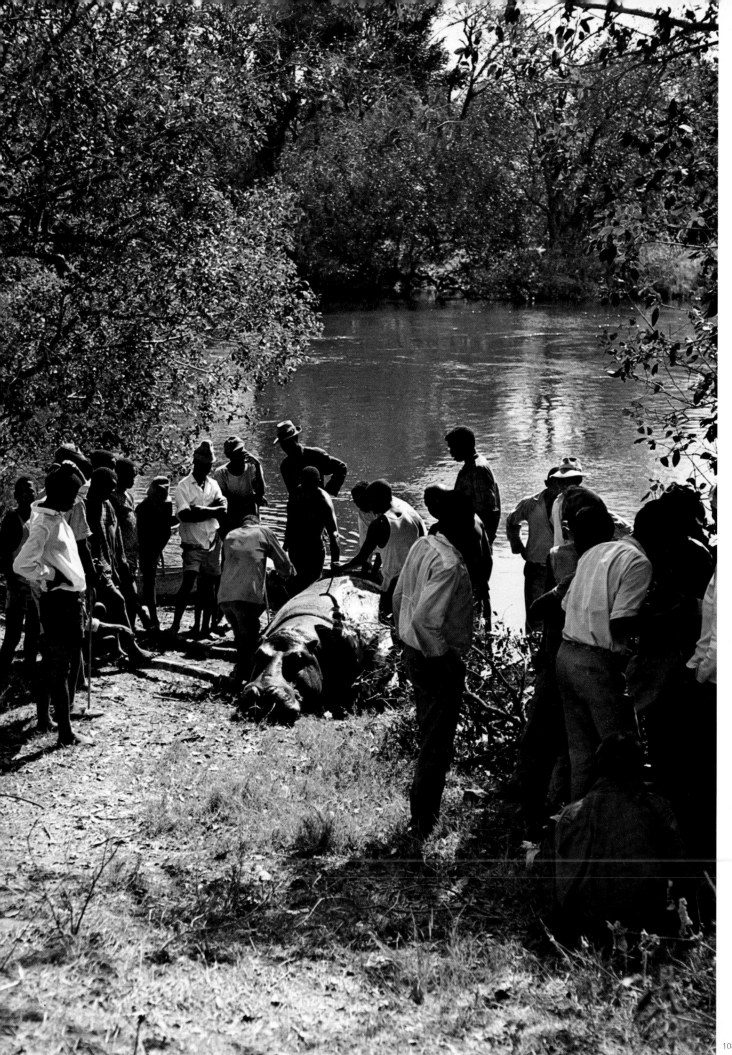

109a

109b

109c

109d

110. The singing and dancing goes on well into the night.

111. The witchdoctor has as much fun as any other at the feast.

112. The children try to imitate their parents. They have a natural sense of rhythm.

113. Young girls join in the clapping and singing

114. This young boy tries a few dance steps.

115a. Granny joins in the fun, her wrinkled face lit up with pleasure.

115b. Boys and girls join in the fun.

116. A man dances and sings exhuberantly . . .

117. . . . while the women watch.

117

118. This woman's wealth is apparent from the number of buttons, beads and bangles she wears.

119. A young woman enjoys the singing.

120a. Dawn has hardly broken when the village girls reach the river with their fishing baskets.

120b. The first rays of sun touch the Kavango river, and the early morning mists rise lazily off the water. Another day has dawned in this beautiful land.